G000048074

This edition copyright © 1997 Lion Publishing
Published by
Lion Publishing plc
Sandy Lane West, Oxford, England
ISBN 0 7459 3874 4
Albatross Books Pty Ltd
PO Box 320, Sutherland, NSW 2232, Australia
ISBN 0 7324 1733 3
First edition 1997
10 9 8 7 6 5 4 3 2 1 0

Text: Extracts from the Authorized Version of
the Bible (The King James Bible), the rights in
which are vested in the Crown, are reproduced
by permission of the Crown's Patentee,
Cambridge University Press.

Pictures: The Bodleian Library, Oxford: MS
Douce 144, fols. 122v–123r; MS Douce 14,
fols. 126r two details; MS Rawl. liturg. f. 26,
fols 55v and 161r; MSS Douce 219–220, fol.
145v; MS Rawl. liturg. f. 26, fol. 69v (cover
picture) by permission of the Warden and
Fellows of Keble College, Oxford: MS 49, fol.
64v.

Artwork: Amanda Barlow

A catalogue record for this book is
available from the British Library

Printed and bound in Singapore

Acknowledgments

We would like to thank all those who have
given us permission to include quotations in
this book. Every effort has been made to trace
and acknowledge copyright holders of all the
quotations. We apologize for any errors or
omissions that may remain, and would ask those
concerned to contact the publishers, who will
ensure that full acknowledgment is made in the
future.

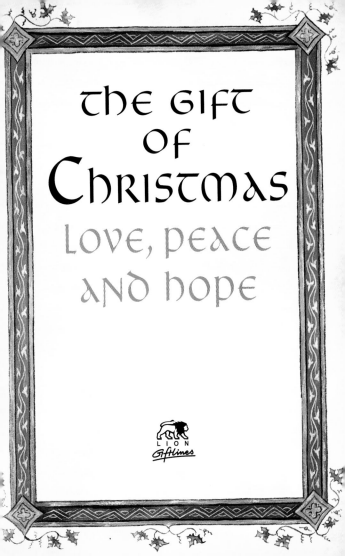

THE GIFT OF CHRISTMAS

LOVE, PEACE AND HOPE

LION
Giftlines

Oulce dame de mise
ricorde mer de pitie
fontaine de tous bi
ens qui portastes nre saigneur
ihucrist ix. mois en uie precieu

INTRODUCTION

The story of Christmas
is at once familiar and
yet constantly new as
we encounter it year by
year. In childhood it is
inextricably linked to
the tingling excitement
of a magic time. And
in later life it still has
the power to warm our
hearts and inspire us.
May this Christmas
once again bring you
the greatest gifts of all
—love, peace and hope
f o r   t h e   f u t u r e.

'There came wise men from
the east... they presented unto
him gifts; gold, and
frankincense,
and myrrh.'

FROM MATTHEW'S GOSPEL

CONTENTS

Given, not lent,
And not withdrawn—once sent,
This Infant of mankind, this One,
Is still the little welcome Son.

New every year,
New born and newly dear,
He comes with tidings and a song,
The ages long, the ages long;

Even as the cold
Keen winter grows not old,
As childhood is so fresh, foreseen,
And spring in the familiar green.

Sudden as sweet
Come the expected feet.
All joy is young, and new all art,
And he, too, whom we have by heart.

ALICE MEYNELL

THE
BIRTH
FORETOLD

Behold, a virgin shall conceive,
and bear a son,
and shall call his name
Immanuel.

*Writing in the 8th century BC, the Old
Testament prophet Isaiah foretells the
birth of Jesus.*

the
story begins

Now the birth of jesus christ was on this wise: when as his mother mary was espoused to joseph, before they came together, she was found with child of the holy ghost.

The Angel Gabriel

The angel Gabriel is one of two archangels mentioned in the Bible (the other is Michael). He first appears in the Book of Daniel in the Old Testament. As God's messenger, Gabriel later appears to Zechariah to tell him the good news about his new son, John, and to Mary to announce the birth of Jesus.

MARY'S SONG

My soul doth magnify the Lord, and my spirit hath rejoiced in God my saviour.

For he hath regarded the low estate of his handmaiden: for, behold, from henceforth all generations shall call me blessed.

For he that is mighty hath done to me great things; and holy is his name.

And his mercy is on them that fear him from generation to generation.

He hath shewed strength

with his arm; he hath scattered
the proud in the imagination of
their hearts.

he hath put down the
mighty from their seats, and
exalted them of low degree.
he hath filled the hungry with
good things; and the rich he
hath sent empty away.

he hath holpen his servant
israel, in remembrance of his
mercy;

as he spake to our fathers,
to abraham, and to his seed for
ever.

A mother's song of praise

*This is Mary's joyous song at the news
that she is to bear God's son. It echoes
the First Book of Samuel in the Old
Testament, where another mother—
Hannah—hears the news that she is
pregnant with her long-hoped-for son.*

JOSEPH AND
THE ANGEL

THEN JOSEPH HER HUSBAND,
BEING A JUST MAN AND NOT
WILLING TO MAKE HER A PUBLICK
EXAMPLE, WAS MINDED TO PUT HER
AWAY PRIVILY.

BUT WHILE HE THOUGHT ON
THESE THINGS, BEHOLD, THE ANGEL
OF THE LORD APPEARED UNTO HIM
IN A DREAM, SAYING, JOSEPH, THOU
SON OF DAVID, FEAR NOT TO TAKE
UNTO THEE MARY THY WIFE; FOR
THAT WHICH IS CONCEIVED IN HER IS
OF THE HOLY GHOST.

AND SHE SHALL BRING FORTH A

SON, AND THOU SHALT CALL HIS NAME JESUS: FOR HE SHALL SAVE HIS PEOPLE FROM THEIR SINS...

THEN JOSEPH BEING RAISED FROM SLEEP DID AS THE ANGEL OF THE LORD HAD BIDDEN HIM, AND TOOK UNTO HIM HIS WIFE:

AND KNEW HER NOT TILL SHE HAD BROUGHT FORTH HER FIRSTBORN SON: AND HE CALLED HIS NAME JESUS.

What's in a name?

The name Jesus is the Greek form of Joshua, and means 'Yahweh (or God) is salvation'. It was a popular name in the 1st century AD. Joshua was the Old Testament hero who led the people of Israel into the promised land. The description of Jesus as the Saviour comes from the meaning of his name as well as his mission.

TO BETHLEHEM

AND IT CAME TO PASS IN THOSE DAYS, THAT THERE WENT OUT A DECREE FROM CÆSAR AUGUSTUS, THAT ALL THE WORLD SHOULD BE TAXED...

AND ALL WENT TO BE TAXED, EVERY ONE INTO HIS OWN CITY.

AND JOSEPH ALSO WENT UP FROM GALILEE, OUT OF THE CITY OF NAZARETH, INTO JUDÆA, UNTO THE CITY OF DAVID, WHICH IS CALLED BETHLEHEM; (BECAUSE HE WAS OF THE HOUSE AND LINEAGE OF DAVID:)

TO BE TAXED WITH MARY HIS ESPOUSED WIFE, BEING GREAT WITH CHILD.

And so it was, that, while they were there, the days were accomplished that she should be delivered.

And she brought forth her first-born son, and wrapped him in swaddling clothes, and laid him in a manger; because there was no room for them in the inn.

the shepherds

And there were in the same country shepherds abiding in the field, keeping watch over their flock by night.

And, lo, the angel of the Lord came upon them, and the glory of the Lord shone round about them: and they were sore afraid.

And the angel said unto them, Fear not: for, behold, I bring you good tidings of great joy, which shall be to all people.

For unto you is born this day in the city of David a saviour, which is Christ the Lord.

And this shall be a sign unto you; ye shall find the babe wrapped in swaddling clothes, lying in a manger.

And suddenly there was with the angel a multitude of the heavenly host praising God, and saying,

Glory to God in the highest, and on earth peace, good will toward men.

I saw a stable,
low and very bare,
A little child in a manger.
The oxen knew him,
had him in their care,
To men he was a stranger.
The safety of the world
was lying there,
and the world's danger.

MARY COLERIDGE

It came upon the midnight clear,
That glorious song of old,
from angels bending near
the earth
To touch their harps of gold:
'Peace on the earth,
good will to men,
From heaven's all-gracious King!'
The world in solemn stillness lay
to hear the angels sing.

Still through the cloven skies
they come,
With peaceful wings unfurled;
And still their heavenly
music floats
O'er all the weary world;
Above its sad and lowly plains
They bend on hovering wing;
And ever o'er its Babel sounds
The blessèd angels sing.

E. H. SEARS

TO FIND THE BABY

AND IT CAME TO PASS, AS THE ANGELS WERE GONE AWAY FROM THEM INTO HEAVEN, THE SHEPHERDS SAID ONE TO ANOTHER, LET US NOW GO EVEN UNTO BETHLEHEM, AND SEE THIS THING WHICH IS COME TO PASS, WHICH THE LORD HATH MADE KNOWN UNTO US.

AND THEY CAME WITH HASTE, AND FOUND MARY, AND JOSEPH, AND THE BABE LYING IN A MANGER.

AND WHEN THEY HAD SEEN IT, THEY MADE KNOWN ABROAD THE SAYING WHICH WAS TOLD THEM CONCERNING THIS CHILD.

AND ALL THEY THAT HEARD IT WONDERED AT THOSE THINGS WHICH WERE TOLD THEM BY THE SHEPHERDS.

BUT MARY KEPT ALL THESE THINGS, AND PONDERED THEM IN HER HEART.

AND THE SHEPHERDS RETURNED, GLORIFYING AND PRAISING GOD FOR ALL THE THINGS THAT THEY HAD HEARD AND SEEN, AS IT WAS TOLD UNTO THEM.

The
Birthplace

But thou, Bethlehem Ephratah,
though thou be little
among the thousands of Judah,
yet out of thee shall he come
forth unto me that is to be
ruler in Israel; whose goings
forth have been from of old,
from everlasting.

These are the words of the Old Testament prophet Micah as he foretells Jesus' birthplace.

THE JOURNEY

Now when Jesus was born in Bethlehem of Judæa in the days of Herod the king, behold, there came wise men from the east to Jerusalem,

saying, Where is he that is born King of the Jews? for we have seen his star in the east, and are come to worship him.

When Herod the king had heard these things, he was troubled, and all Jerusalem with him.

And when he had gathered all the chief priests and scribes of the people together, he demanded of them where christ should be born.

and they said unto him, in bethlehem of judæa: for thus it is written by the prophet,

and thou bethlehem, in the land of juda, art not the least among the princes of juda: for out of thee shall come a governor, that shall rule my people israel.

PRECIOUS GIFTS

Then herod, when he had privily called the wise men, inquired of them diligently what time the star appeared.

And he sent them to bethlehem, and said, go and search diligently for the young child; and when ye have found him, bring me word again, that I may come and worship him also.

When they had heard the king, they departed; and, lo, the star, which they saw in the east, went before them, till it came and stood over where the young child was.